Out of Spain

Book I: Ayer – Our Spanish Heritage

**Five lessons covering the history of the Jews of Spain prior to their expulsion in 1492
Optional addition to Book 1: a 12-minute teaching video**

Lessons created and written by Yvonne Behar, B.A. (Hons.) LRAM, ARCM

Edited and directed by Andrée Aelion Brooks
Graphic design: Yvonne Behar/Andrée Aelion Brooks
Video/Craig Davidson for Refocus Films
Curriculum advisers: Rabbi Robert Orkand
and Mark Casso, Director of Education,
both with Temple Israel of Westport, CT.
Historical consultant: Prof. Jane Gerber
Copy editing/proof reading: Wilbur Hollander
Grants provided by: the Maurice Amado
Foundation and United Jewish Appeal of
Westport, Weston, Wilton, Norwalk, CT.
Seed money provided by Andrée Aelion Brooks

ACKNOWLEDGMENTS

This curriculum would have never been completed without the generous and thoughtful assistance of a number of specialists and friends who came forward to offer advice, sources, ideas, private libraries, personal recollections. Our special thanks to Professor Yom Tov Assis of Hebrew University in Jerusalem, whose lectures at Yale and in Holland Park Synagogue in London helped to provide a contextual background; George Anticoni, also of London, who gave us access to his unique collection of books and tapes on Sephardic topics and was always on hand to give advice; Claudia Roden, the distinguished food writer who permitted us to draw on her special knowledge on Sephardic cuisine.

In addition, we would like thank Georgette Behar for her help and encouragement; Flory Jagoda who gave permission for her wonderful Ladino songs; Hillary Pomeroy whose conferences at London University provided a rich source of material and ideas; Yvonne's husband, Laurie, and children, Juliette and Anna, who did without endless meals; Rosalind Anticoni, for her recipes and memories of family Seders; the Maurice Amado Foundation for its generous support and keen interest in our work; Sarah Lascar and Pamela Kesselman for their personal belief in the value of our project; the wise counsel of Jane Gerber and the late Seymour Mund, whose willingness to take on any task and his patient support made it all possible.

ABOUT THE CREATIVE TEAM:

Project Director: **Andrée Aelion Brooks** is a journalist, author, teacher and lecturer. Ms. Brooks is a former contributing columnist and a feature writer for *The New York Times* and author of the award-winning book, "Children of Fast-Track Parents" (Viking, 1989). She is also an Associate Fellow, Yale University. Ms. Brooks, who regularly writes and lectures to community groups on Jewish history, comes from a Sephardic background. She has also been working on an allied project – a biography of Doña Gracia Nasi, the 16th century Jewish woman banker and *converso* leader.

Curriculum producer: **Yvonne Behar** is a teacher with 20 years of classroom experience and a curriculum specialist. Ms. Behar, who also comes from a Sephardic family, is widely known for her expertise in Sephardic music and culture. She has taught courses at the university level in Sephardic history and culture and regularly travels to Spain to lecture on these topics to visiting study groups. She has designed and implemented interactive curriculum materials for schools and summer camps and has been praised by school officials for her imaginative teaching methods.

Video producer: **Craig Davidson** is an independent video documentary producer and winner of many awards. He has created productions for CNN, PBS, Fox and HBO, some of which have also covered aspects of Jewish history.

Historical consultant: **Prof. Jane Gerber** is the director of the Institute for Sephardic Studies at City University of New York and author of the award-winning book, "The Jews of Spain," (1992).

Project Committee: **Rabbi Robert Orkand** is the senior rabbi of Temple Israel, Westport CT and a former chairman of the National Commission on Reform Jewish Education. **Mark Casso** is the director of Temple Israel Religious School.

MORE INFORMATION:

write: Andrée Aelion Brooks
Hitchcock Books
15 Hitchcock Road
Westport, CT 06880   U.S.A
Phone: 203- 226-9834
Fax: 203-226-0814
E-mail: andreebrooks@hotmail.com

A Production of Hitchcock Books in conjunction with Temple Israel, Westport, CT
Copyright © 2000 AndréeAelion Brooks

Table of Contents

Book 1: Spain before the Expulsion

Introduction..7

Lesson 1. Who are the Sephardic Jews? An historical introduction that includes *Ayer: Our Spanish Heritage* a 12-minute video prepared for this curriculum................9

Lesson 2. The Great Invasion: the impact of the arrival of the Moors in Spain......................................13

Lesson 3. Heroes of the Golden Age and Beyond: poets, songs, medicine and science...........................19

*****Lesson 4.** Music in the Castles: birth of the Romanza and favorite instruments...26

Lesson 5. Expulsion or Conversion: All about the Great Expulsion of 1492...31

*an audiotape is available to accompany this lesson

INTRODUCTION

To understand more about our ancestors, we need to learn more about how Jews in general lived in centuries past. This series traces the history of the multitude of Jews whose ancestors came from the Iberian peninsula. Many had lived there since ancient times, helping to develop and rule the land until the Spanish monarchs, Ferdinand and Isabella, expelled them in 1492; the same year that Columbus set sail for the Americas. But they couldn't erase their Spanish heritage. Over the centuries these Iberian Jews had developed a culture very different from the northern European or Ashkenazi Jews. They took that culture into exile. They are important because they represent one of the largest segments of the Jewish people, including perhaps some students in your class.

The series tells what happened to these Spanish or Sephardic Jews during their time on the Iberian peninsula and afterwards; a period too often overlooked in Jewish history. It recreates their adventures, sorrows and achievements before and after they were forced out. It looks at their music, language, food, songs, customs and folk tales and provides a glimpse of their lives in Spain.

Some real life stories are included. You will meet Doña Gracia Nasi who used her fortune to help the Jews escape from the neighboring country of Portugal. And when you have played the Caribbean adventure game and met Carla, the ship's cat, you will understand how and why some of the earliest Jews came to the Americas.

Today, Sephardic Jews live in all parts of the world and still practice many of their original Spanish customs. Whether they reside in Istanbul, Amsterdam, Curaçao, London, Seattle, Tel Aviv, San Paulo or New York, they all share a common cultural heritage that binds them together in laughter, food, music and song.

There is an old legend that says that when the Jews were expelled from Spain, they took along the old rusty keys to their houses to remind them of the life they loved in Spain. Although most families no longer have these keys, they became a symbol of their unique heritage and common history that harkens back to Spain.

...here is their story

MAP OF SOUTHERN EUROPE

Lesson 1

WHO ARE THE SEPHARDIC JEWS?

Task 1

Watch the video introduction to the story of the Sephardic Jews.

Afterwards – discuss as a class

1. In the video, the grandfather explained to the children why his family is Sephardic and not Ashkenazi. What did he say?
   ....
   ....

   > **Ashkenazi** is the name given to Jews from Northern and Eastern Europe

2. The grandfather mentioned that when the Arab Muslims invaded Spain they shared their knowledge of science with the Jews. What other knowledge did they share?………………………………………

3. When the Christians re-conquered Spain, some of the Jews held official positions in the castles and cities. Can you name one of the jobs they did?
   ……………………………………………

4. The grandfather said that 1492 was a "horrible time" for the Jews. What did he mean?
   ……………………………………………………………………………

5. The children were singing a Hanukkah song called Ocho Kandelikas. What language were the children using in the song?
   ……………………………………………………………………………

6. Where did the grandfather's family go before coming to America?
   ………………………………………………………………..

Task 2: **Discuss as a class**

7. Do you know where your family originally came from?………..

8. Do you know any Sephardic families? Where did *they* come from?
   ……………………………………………………………………………

9

Task 3:

Find Spain on a world map and then on a map of Europe. Compare its location with Israel at the other end of the Mediterranean Sea.

Then…. complete the chart on the next page. You will see that it has room for eight explanatory paragraphs. Three have already been inserted. The others are not yet there. They are listed below. Working in pairs, read through the passages below and match them with the illustrations on the left side of the chart. Copy them onto the right side in the appropriate boxes.

When the Roman Empire collapsed the warrior tribes that overran Spain were called Visigoths. They tried to convert the Jews to Christianity.

Finally, when the Christian soldiers took the last Muslim stronghold of Granada early in 1492, King Ferdinand and Queen Isabella decided to expel the Jews. Only those Jews who agreed to convert to Christianity could stay. The rest had only four months to leave.

Jews had been living in Spain since the days of the Roman Empire. Today, Jews whose ancestors came from Spain are known as Sephardic Jews.

Legend insists that many took along the old rusty keys to their houses to remind them of their life in Spain. They also kept those memories alive in language, song and food. As their culture and roots had come from Spain they were known forever afterwards as Sephardim.

Years later, many of these Sephardic Jews who had originally resettled in lands around the Mediterranean or other parts of Europe found their way to America.

THE JEWS FROM SPAIN

Spain 100-300AD	
Visigoths 586AD	
Muslim Invasion 711AD	Not long after, things improved. The next invaders were the Arabs and Berbers from North Africa. They were Muslims. At that time the Muslims were friends of the Jews. Afterwards, for hundreds of glorious years the Muslims ruled over much of Spain. During this time scientific, medical, poetic and literary skills of the Jews fused with advanced Arabic learning. Moorish architecture, copied by the Jews, enhanced the landscape of Spain.
Reconquest 1037-1492	Later a religious Muslim sect came to power that no longer tolerated the Jews. But by then the Jews were welcomed by the knights and lords who lived in the castles that dotted the Christian parts of Spain. The Christian kings had begun to push the Muslim Arabs back out of Spain and the Jews helped them rebuild new cities and repopulate cities abandoned by Muslims. These battles took a lot of money that certain Jews helped the Christian kings to collect.
1492 Ferdinand and Isabella	
	Some Jews went on dangerous journeys to other lands, which bordered the Mediterranean. They scattered to Italy, Turkey and North Africa. Others went overland to Portugal where they were later forced to convert against their will. After this happened many fled onwards to Holland, France and the Caribbean.
USA 1654 →	

Additional Task
Names and Places

A. Look at the map of Spain below and **underline** the following cities that were centers of Jewish culture in Medieval times. Sevilla, Granada, Toledo, Tarragona, Barcelona, Salamanca, Bejar, Zaragoza, Lucena, Caceres and Cordoba. Even today, some Sephardic Jews have family names that refer to towns where their Spanish ancestors lived.

B. Study these family names on the left of the box below. Then insert the names of the towns where you think the following people might have come from. Enter the town name at the star* in the empty box on the right.

Suzanne Toledano	*
Maurice Saragossi	*
Michel Cordova	*
Sylvia Tarragano	*
Abraham de Lucena	*
Esther de Caceres	*
Coco Sevilla	*

Lesson 2
THE GREAT INVASION

Jews first arrived on the Spanish peninsula in biblical times. They continued to prosper there even after the Romans conquered the region. But in the 5th century a warrior tribe called the Visigoths swept down from the north and severely persecuted the Jews. The Visigoths were Catholics and insisted Jews become Catholic too. When the Jews resisted, the Visigoths tried to make them into slaves and prevented them from communicating with Jews in other countries.

But this was about to change…..

Two centuries later, in 711, the Muslim Arabs (the Moors) came across the sea from northwest Africa pushing out the Visigoths, who then fled north in fear. Eventually, the only part of Spain still controlled by the Visigoths were the towns and cities in the far north.

Read the following story………. It tells what happened when the conquering Muslim armies reached the great city of Cordoba.

One night the skies became overcast and the rains came followed by hail. The guards on the wall took cover from the weather and abandoned their rounds. The Moors took advantage of the darkness, crossing the river at a shallow point. The southern wall of the city was built some fifteen yards from the river's edge. When Mughith's men (the Muslims) arrived on the other side of the river they went to where there was a gap high up in the wall. A fig tree grew near the gap. Quickly they climbed the tree and sprang onto the wall. The first man drew the second one up after him, and within moments a group of men stood on the wall. Immediately they dropped down inside, fell on the surprised guards of the nearest gate and killed them. They opened the gate. Then through it, with drawn swords, streamed the rest of the forces of Mughith.

Here and there an individual tried to resist – only to be beheaded. Most of the people barred the doors of their houses and remained quietly within. However, the governor escaped with his forces to a church and they barricaded themselves inside. On the following morning when the people of Cordoba came out of their houses they saw that Mughith had occupied the governor's palace. They knew they had lost. The Jews of the city, on the other hand, were delighted. This was the day they had hoped for. They immediately made contact with the Muslim officer who asked them to join his army and they had the job of guarding the city.
(from The Jews of Muslim Spain by Eliyahu Ashtor)

Task 1

<u>Answer the following questions</u>

1. *When did the Muslim invasion of Spain take place?*......................................
2. *How did they get into the city?*..
....
3. *What was the name of the city?*...
4. *What did the Jews do?*
....
5. *Why had the Jews been unhappy before the Muslims arrived?*
....

After the invasion the Muslims gave the Jews new freedoms

The text you have just read illustrates how the Jews helped guard certain cities for the Muslim Arabs when they invaded Spain in 711. The Jews were loyal to their new rulers. The Muslim Arabs repaid them by:

giving them freedom of worship
giving them more important jobs
permitting them to study
allowing them to travel and trade freely

Now that the Jews were free to practice their religion, they made contact with the Jewish rabbis in Bagdad who they held in high respect. They could get advice on matters of religion and Jewish law.

Now that the Jews were free to develop their skills as traders, they organized expeditions to Africa and the Eastern Mediterranean and brought back spices, papyrus, textiles, oils and wines.

The Jews were now free to study many languages. They already used Hebrew for their prayers, and spoke an early form of Spanish. Now they could openly learn Arabic, Latin and Greek and were in great demand as translators.

They could even own land, provided they paid extra taxes for the privilege.

The Muslim Invasion also had a great cultural impact

After the Muslim invasion the Jews were encouraged to study and develop their skills. As a result, a great exchange of knowledge took place in the fields of science and the arts between the Jews and the Muslims.

Poetry, music, food and architecture became infused with both Jewish and Arabic influences.

The Jews who worked at the royal courts of the Muslim rulers learned that if they acquired a good knowledge of Arabic poetry and literature it could allow them to hold more important positions. By the 10th century, as a result of the Arabic influence, a new form of Hebrew poetry emerged that used Arabic forms and was not necessarily concerned with religious topics.

Jewish musicians came into contact with highly accomplished lute players and harpists. Similarly, they began to borrow popular Arabic tunes for their own hymns and love songs.

For hundreds of years, some of the favorite foods cooked by the Jews, such as the Sabbath stew called Adafina, which uses chick peas, nuts and aromatic herbs and spices, further reflected the influence of these North African Arabs.

The Arabs built glorious mosques and palaces in the Moorish style such as the Great Mosque in Cordoba, constructed in 796 and still standing. It has a forest of arches. It has arabesque designs of leaves and plants intertwined with decorative writing. This style of architecture lasted for hundreds of years and became an inspiration for Jewish architecture. For example, the Jews built the Transito Synagogue in Toledo in 1376 using shapes and decorations in the Moorish style.

Arches and decorations

The Moorish style was the name of architectural style used by the Muslims to build their mosques and palaces.

The Muslims were followers of Islam, the Muslim religion. This meant that Spain now became part of the great Islamic Empire that stretched east almost as far as China. The architecture of the Muslims reflected a mixture of all the countries they had conquered including Persia, Turkey and parts of Mongolia.

The Jews lived alongside the Muslims in many of the cities in Spain. They were impressed by these beautiful shapes and decorations. They began to use them for their synagogues.

Task 2: **Observation and Discussion**

Look at the illustration (below left) of the **Alhambra Palace**. It was built originally for the Muslim kings of Granada in Spain.

The Alhambra Palace   El Transito Synagogue

Find: Horseshoe-shaped arches
Scalloped arches
Carved lace design on the windows
Arabic writing (calligraphy) used decoratively
Arabesque design (leaves and flowers)

Now look at the illustration to the right. It shows the **El Transito** synagogue in the Spanish city of **Toledo. El Transito** is still there today and you can visit it when you next go to Spain.

1. Which shapes and decorations are the same?
2. What is different that tells you it is a synagogue?

Now think about synagogues built in your own community or region. Have they been designed to look like other the public buildings or houses? Do they remind you of the way the Spanish Jews designed El Transito to look like the buildings being constructed by *their* Muslim neighbors?

Discuss the following:
How have your synagogues been affected by local architectural styles?
Do they echo the shapes used by other buildings?
Are the synagogues built with the same local materials?
How might they be different and why?

Task 3 : Complete the following designs found in synagogues in Spain:

1. A horseshoe shape arch

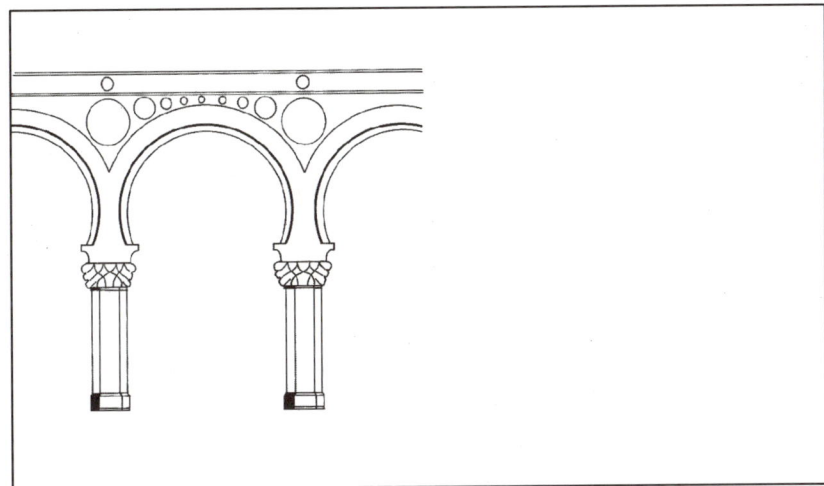

2. A scalloped arch

3. An arabesque design

4. Invent your own Hebrew inscription. Write it the space above the arches.

All sketches by Graham Charles Stone

Optional Task 4: Using a separate sheet of blank paper design your own interior wall for a synagogue in Spain, using a combination of arches, arabesque design and Hebrew inscription. Color it in pink, yellow and green.

Lesson 3 *The Flowering of a Golden Age*

Many different groups of people exist in this world, each with its own special culture. People are shaped by their own experiences as well as the ideas they pick up from those outside their own group. Understanding how a culture develops helps us learn more about the sources of Jewish heritage.

The years following the Muslim invasion of Spain in 711 were golden ones for the Jews. Their study of poetry, science and philosophy was enlivened by contact with the vibrant Moorish culture that had swept over most of Spain. The only part of Spain unaffected by the invasion was a small section of the northwest that had not been conquered by the Muslims. This became known as Christian Spain. But very few Jews lived in that part of the country, at least in the beginning. So most Jews were deeply affected by the Muslim culture.

The Muslim rulers used the ancient city of Cordoba as their capital (*locate Cordoba on the map of Spain*). To display their power, they built great palaces and mosques in a sumptuous style with shaped arches and arabesque designs.

At this time the Muslims were more advanced scientifically than the Christians. They understood irrigation. They knew how to build a strong agricultural economy and a flourishing silk trade. They were so prosperous that the nobles and courtiers working at the palace could wear luxurious clothes of fine silk.

The Jews helped to enrich this economy by becoming successful traders and silk merchants. They also traded in herbs and spices, many of them from other Muslim lands. As a result they developed a keen knowledge of herbal remedies. This was one reason why Jewish doctors became so popular.

The wealthy Muslim rulers encouraged the spirit of learning among all of their peoples. They considered the study of science and perfection of language the path to advancement. They became patrons of learning, willing to pay for the best scholars – whether Muslims, Christians or Jews – to bring them the latest scientific and philosophical ideas. As the Jews were now encouraged to write books and study languages, many became fluent in Arabic, Hebrew, Aramaic and Spanish (then called Romance). No wonder they were in demand as translators and overseas representatives. They had quickly developed a high standard of literacy.

> **Patron**: someone who helps you do something creative by giving money

The ability to speak eloquently and write good poetry was also highly prized by the Muslim leaders. They were prepared to pay well for poets to write suitable verse for every occasion. Poems were written for family events, to flatter friends or insult enemies.

As a result, the Jews looked to their own language and wanted to perfect Hebrew poetry too. Today, prayer books contain great prayers and poems written at this time by Jewish poets such as Yehuda Halevi, Ibn Gabirol and Dunash ibn Labrat.

Ibn means "son of" and has Arabic origins.

One special man is credited with launching the Golden Age

There was one particular Jew living in Spain during this period. He was a doctor and a linguist. He was also head of the Jewish community and founder of a Talmudic academy. Many consider that it was he who launched the Golden Age of culture for the Jews of Spain. His name was Hasdai Shaprut.

Hasdai had shown unusual ability as a doctor. When he announced that he had discovered a cure for poisons he was appointed personal physician to one of the Muslim rulers. This enabled him to work at the great palace in Cordoba. While there, he helped to translate an important medical manuscript called *De Materia Medica* by Dioscorides. This allowed the city of Cordoba to function as a scientific center. Students no longer had to go abroad for medical study. Hasdai Shaprut's many talents helped him rise to a position of power and influence. Here is a story that illustrates how he did so:

One day he heard that Sancho the Fat, a Christian king in the far northern part of Spain, wanted his help. Sancho was so fat that he could not ride his horse and needed help to walk. Consequently, Sancho had become an object of ridicule. One day he woke up to find he had been ousted from power and someone else had been put on his throne. So Sancho went to his grandmother, Queen Toda, asking for help. She decided he needed military assistance from the Muslims to gain back his throne. He also needed a good doctor to cure his obesity. Imagine a Christian Queen arriving to ask a Muslim ruler (who had been her enemy) for help and seeking advice from a Jewish doctor! In the end Hasdai cured Sancho with a mixture of exercise and herbs. A Muslim army was then dispatched and Sancho regained his throne.

Hasdai won much admiration. Now he was able to realize his greater ambitions. He had a dream that Jewish learning and culture should become as important as

Muslim culture. He therefore decided to import sacred and scientific books from other countries so they could be studied by the Jews of Spain. He also maintained a correspondence with the great Talmudic schools in Bagdad and paid talented Jewish scholars around him to write poetry.

Suddenly Jewish poets began to expand their writings. Instead of limiting their work to prayers and hymns for the synagogue, they also wrote about wine, love or great deeds. One of the popular subjects for poetry was praise for your patron. Dunash ben Labrat, one of the most **innovative** poets of the time, wrote this poem in praise of Hasdai Shaprut and how he cured Sancho the Fat.

Task 1.
A. Can you work out what Hasdai negotiated for curing Sancho and sending in the Muslim army?
Hint: it's somewhere near the beginning…

> Are you **innovative**? You are if you have a lot of new ideas that you are not afraid to try out.

Celebratory Song – by Dunash ben Labrat

Compose a song of praise
In honor of our Prince, head of the Academy
Who totally destroyed the foreign forces.
He is girded with glory and majesty
Invested with divine assistance.
He snatched ten fortresses from the insolents *(Christians)*
And wrought havoc
Among the thorns and thistles.

He brought Ramiro's son *(Sancho)*
Princes and priests.
Lord, knight and king
He brought like a pawn
Scepter in hand
to an enemy people;

He also dragged the simple,
ancient Toda,
Who wore her royalty
Just like a man.
With the strength of his wisdom
With the power of his astuteness
With the multitude of his subtleties
And the sweetness of his words.

B. What sort of a woman was Queen Toda?..
C. Which lines praise Hasdai's character the most?............................
D. Lines 4 and 5 liken Hasdai's personal qualities to............................

In those days it was very fashionable to write poems of praise. Poets were rather like publicists today, spreading the word about your good character and achievements.

Do you think you perform better when you are praised? ....
Can you name two skills that you deserve praise for?..............................
Do you know of any local people who are patrons?................................

After Hasdai Shaprut died, other rabbis, poets and philosophers followed in his footsteps. One of these was Samuel Nagrella. He was very unusual because he became an assistant to the ruler of Granada as well as a commander in the Muslim army. He wrote many poems while on the battlefield. They give a vivid description of his difficult life. As they did not have TV or films in those days, poetry had to stimulate the imagination.

Samuel makes his descriptions of the battlefield more powerful by describing colors, sound and movement.

Task 2. Take turns reading a section of the poem below and then discuss your impressions.

An excerpt from Nagrella's poem about the Battle of Alfuente

> The earth's foundations, overthrown like Gomorrah, reeled to and fro.
> Every face turned red or black as the bottom of a pot.
> It was a day of darkness and thick fog.
> The sun was as black as my heart.
> The tumult was like that of a cloudburst, like the roar of breakers when the sea is swept by a storm. As the sun came out, the earth rocked on its pillars as if it were drunk.
> The horses lunged back and forth like vipers darting out of their nests.
> The hurled spears were like bolts of lighting, filling the air with light.
> Arrows pelted us like raindrops, as if our shields were sieves.
> Their strung bows were like serpents, each serpent spewing forth a stinging bee.
> Their swords above their heads were like glowing torches which darken as they fall.
> The blood of men flowed upon the ground like the blood of rams on the corners of the altar.

Religious prayers and songs

If you open any prayer book you will find the services enriched by poems and prayers written by rabbis and poets living during this period. For example, you may have sung *Mi Chamochah* by Judah Halevi or *El Nora Alila* by Moses ibn Ezra at Yom Kippur.

Task 3: Work out how Judah Halevi puts his signature on the song, *Mi Chamochah,* by looking at the this song.

Disregard the title and the first two lines.
Then count the verses…………………….
Underline the first Hebrew letter of each verse and write them down from right to left…………………………………..
Pronounce the word these letters make.
How do we know this song is by Judah Halevi?………………

Mi Chamochah

Who is like You, revealing the deeps,
   fearful in praises, doing wonders?

The creator who discovers all from nothing
is revealed to the heart, but not to the eye;
therefore ask not how nor where—
   for He fills heaven and earth.

Remove lust from the midst of you;
you will find your God within you,
walking gently in your heart.
   He who brings low and lifts up.

And see the way of the soul's secret,
search it out and refresh yourself.
He will make you wise, and you will find freedom,
   for you are a captive and the world is a prison.

Make knowledge the envoy between yourself and Him.
Annul your will and do His will,
and know that wherever you hide, there is His eye,
   and nothing is too hard for Him.

He was the Living One, while there was yet no dust of the world,
and He is the maker and He the bearer,
and man is counted as a fading flower—
   soon to fade, as fades a leaf.

מִי כָמוֹךָ

מִי כָמוֹךָ עֲמָקוֹת גִּלָּה
נוֹרָא תְהִלֹּת עֹשֵׂה־פֶלֶא:

יוֹצֵר הַמַּמְצִיא כֹּל מֵאַיִן נִגְלֶה לַלֵּבָב לֹא לָעָיִן
כֵּן אַל־תִּשְׁאַל אֵיךְ וְאָיִן כִּי שָׁמַיִם וָאָרֶץ מָלֵא:

הָסֵר תַּאֲוָה מִקִּרְבְּךָ תִּמְצָא צוּרְךָ תּוֹךְ חַבְּךָ
מִתְהַלֵּךְ לְאַט בִּלְבָבְךָ הוּא הַמּוֹרִיד וְהוּא הַמַּעֲלֶה:

וּרְאֵה דֶרֶךְ סוֹד הַנֶּפֶשׁ וַחֲקֹר אֹתָהּ וּבָהּ תִּנָּפֵשׁ
הוּא יַשְׂכִּילְךָ וְתִמְצָא חֹפֶשׁ כִּי אַתְּ אָסִיר וְעוֹלָם כֶּלֶא:

דַּעַת שִׂים צִיר בֵּינְךָ וּבֵינוֹ וּבַטֵּל רְצוֹנְךָ וַעֲשֵׂה רְצוֹנוֹ
וְדַע כִּי בַאֲשֶׁר תַּסְתִּיר עֵינוֹ וְדָבָר מִמֶּנּוּ לֹא־יִפָּלֵא:

הוּא הַחַי בְּאֵין עַפְרוֹת תֵּבֵל וְהוּא הָעֹשֶׂה וְהוּא הַסֹּבֵל
וְאָדָם נֶחְשַׁב כְּצִיצַת נָבֵל יְבוֹל מַהֵר כִּנְבֹל עָלֶה:

THE PHILOSOPHER MAIMONIDES

Statue of Maimonides in Maimonides Square in Cordoba, Spain

Maimonides was one of the greatest thinkers of the Golden Age. As well as being a philosopher and a religious leader, he also wrote books on astronomy and practiced medicine.

He grew up under difficult circumstances. He was born in Cordoba where he first studied science and medicine. When he was only 13, Cordoba was taken over by fanatic Muslims called Almohades. Even though his family fled to Morocco they were unable to live openly as Jews. Eventually he finally settled in Cairo. There he became doctor to the Sultan, but he also felt deeply that he should not neglect his duty to the members of his own Jewish community. We can get an idea of his busy daily life from a letter he sent to his friend Samuel ibn Tibbon who lived in Spain:

"I dwell in Misr (Fustat) and the Sultan resides in Cairo; these two places are two Sabbath days journey distant from each other. My duties to the Sultan are very heavy. I am obliged to visit him every day, early in the morning; and when he or any of his children, or any of the inmates of his harem, are indisposed, I dare not quit Cairo, but must stay during the greater part of the day in the palace. It also frequently happens that one or two of the royal officers fall sick, and I must attend to their healing. Hence, as a rule, I repair to Cairo very early in the day and even if nothing unusual happens, I do not return to Fustat until the afternoon. Then I am almost dying of hunger….I find the antechambers filled with people, both Jews and Gentiles, nobles and common people, judges and bailiffs, friends and foes – a mixed multitude who await the time of my return.

I dismount from my animal, wash my hands, go forth to my patients and entreat them to bear with me while I partake of some slight refreshment, the only meal I take in the 24 hours. Then I go forth to my patients, write prescriptions and directions for their several ailments. Patients go in and out until nightfall, and sometimes even, I assure you, until two hours and more during the night. I converse with and prescribe for them while lying down from sheer fatigue; and when night falls, I am so exhausted that I can scarcely speak."

Maimonides is best known to the Jews for organizing the Jewish code of law into a sort of dictionary form. This made it easy to look up whatever you needed to know, such as a rule concerning the eating of certain foods or customs relating to marriage. This work was called his *Mishneh Torah (The Repetition of the Law)*. It took him nine years to complete. It was something nobody had attempted on this scale before. He wrote it to help other Jews continue to practice their religion under difficult conditions.

Many people wrote letters to Maimonides asking for his advice on Jewish legal matters. One of his most famous letters was written to the troubled Jews of Morocco who had been forced to convert to the Muslim faith or die. He told them that if they pretended to convert but privately practiced the Jewish faith at home it was okay as long as they left and went to live in a safer place as soon as they could. He assured them that God would not reject them. Maimonides sympathized with their agonizing predicament and was concerned that the community should have the opportunity to survive.

Maimonides felt that in order to get close to God one had to study philosophy. Not everyone agreed and later on in Spain the rabbis banned his books because they felt that the study of philosophy was a distraction from the study of Judaism.

Today the writings of Maimonides can be found in many prayer books. He wrote 13 principles or articles of faith that have since become famous. Victims of the Nazi Holocaust are known to have gone to their death singing his words. And on Friday nights many congregations around the world sing his *Yigdal*, which is an arrangement of these 13 principles of faith.

Can you find Yigdal in your prayer book? What does it talk about?

Task 4.  Internet Investigation

Use a search engine such as Yahoo.com. look up Maimonides. Then click on the (blue)word RAMBAM. Using what you find on him in general, try to answer the questions below.

1. Why was Maimonides known as Rambam?

2. Where was he born?

3. Who supported him so he could write books and become leader of his community?

4. What did his brother do? How did his brother die?

5. In what language did the Rambam write the Mishneh Torah?

6. Take a look at his writing.

7. What did Maimonides disapprove of using to heal the sick?

6. Find one of his sayings that is meaningful to you? Discuss this with the class.

Lesson 4

MUSIC IN THE CASTLES.... and other DISCOVERIES

Between 1037 and 1492 the Christians gradually re-conquered Spain from the Moors (Muslims from North Africa). As they did so, the new Christian kings gave many Jews high positions at their courts, just as the Muslim rulers had done before them. For example, the Jews were employed as tax collectors. And this helped the Christian rulers to finance their wars. Many educated Jews also spoke fluent Arabic. And this was useful since they could work on translations of important **dispatches** and documents and negotiate with the Moors. By this time, Spanish had become the everyday language of the land.

> **Dispatches** are letters and reports from other kingdoms

One of the most enterprising Christian kings was Alfonso X (1252-1284). Known as "Alfonso the Wise," he had an enthusiasm for learning. He employed Jews as translators, astronomers, physicians, poets and musicians. In fact, at his court, you could find Jewish, Christian and Muslim scholars working together on books. In their spare time they would even share a game of chess. Entertainment would be provided by poets, musicians and entertainers, as well as visiting minstrels from other European countries. They sang and played Arabic instruments such as lutes, bowed fiddles and drums as well as flutes and bagpipes.

Historical documents tell us that at the time of Alfonso's death he had 27 musicians working for him. Among them there was at least one Jewish musician and 13 Muslims. *(pair of drums)*

The attitude towards the Jews at the court was a mixture of tolerance and hostility. Alfonso enjoyed having the successful Jews working for him and earning money for him. At the same time there was mounting pressure to encourage the Jews and Muslims to convert and become Christians too. Cantigas de Santa Maria were songs written at Alfonso's court. These songs suggest that Jews and Muslims could be won over by the force of a miracle and persuaded to convert. Other songs portray the Jews as belonging to the devil. Today, these songs would not be regarded as politically correct.

(lute)

A LUTE AND A FIDDLE

Illustrations of songs written at Alfonso's court show that they used a number of Arabic instruments as well as popular European instruments.

Look at illustration below (A) and notice the long-necked LUTE (or Arabic oud) and also the stringed FIDDLE (Arabic *rebab*) held on the player's lap. The performer draws a bow across the strings of a fiddle to play it. Notice the shape of the bow. How is it different from a violin bow used today?

Other instruments found at Alfonso's court were:
  LONG TRUMPETS   DRUMS   BAGPIPES   FLUTES AND WHISTLES

Suddenly…   similar musical instruments started appearing in a Spanish Haggadah

Task 1. Look below at picture (A-left) of the lute and fiddle. Then look at picture (B-right) from a 14th century Haggadah created in Barcelona, a city in Spain.
Notice the following:
In picture (B) the man seated at the top is holding two matzot. Below him you will see musicians playing instruments like those at Alfonso's court.

Illustration from Cantigas de Santa Maria   **From a 14th century Haggadah from Barcelona**

A   B

Can you find the lute, the bagpipes, the fiddle, the drums, a flute and the long trumpets? Label each instrument you find on the illustration.

27

   Other popular songs sung at this time were ballads or Romanzas. The minstrels sang these songs. They tell fairy tale stories of queens, kings, princesses, love and revenge. Some are about the battles between Christians and Muslims. Others are about girls who fall in love with the sort of boys their parents consider unsuitable. The Jews continued to sing many of these songs to their children for hundreds of years after they had left Spain. Because most could not write, they had to rely upon memory. In this way they were passed down **orally** from generation to generation.

> When parents or grandparents teach their children about family traditions by singing songs or telling stories, it called an **"oral"** tradition. Do you have any in your family?

Task 2   **ACT OUT A BALLAD**

When the Jews left Spain they went to Greece, Turkey and Morocco where they continued to sing the following song. Some of these families later moved to the United States. Even today, there may be a few grandmothers who still know this song. It tells the story of **DIEGO LEÓN**. He is deeply in love with a beautiful girl but her parents do not approve!

1. Listen to the song and then read through the English translation.
2. Then number the verses from 1 through 14

Diego León – a Sephardic Ballad

En la ciudad de Toledo Y en la ciudad de Granada Ahi se criara un mancebo Que Diego León se llama.	In the city of Toledo and in the city of Granada there was born a young man who was called Diego León.
De una tal se enamoró De una muy hermoza dama. Se miran por una reja Tambien por una ventana	In one instant he fell in love with a very beautiful young lady. They saw each other through a grill and through the window.
Un dia que estaban juntos Dijo León a su dama: "Mañana te he de pedir No se si es cosa cercana."	One day when they were together León said to his lady: "Tomorrow I will ask for your hand I don't know whether it will be granted."
"Aunque mi padre no quiera Eso negociado estaba,"	"Even if my father doesn't agree I have already agreed,"
lo que la dama responde Al mozo le agradaba.	is what the young lady said. And the young man was pleased.
Otro dia en la mañana con Don Pedro se encontrara de rodillas en el suelo.	The next day in the morning they met Don Pedro kneeling on the ground.

Los buenos dias le daba:	He greeted him:
"Don Pedro dame a tu hija, A tu hija Doña Juana." "Mi hija no es de cazar Que aun es niña y muchacha."	"Don Pedro give me your daughter's hand, your daughter Dona Juana." "My daughter is not getting married since she is only a child and young."
"Hija León te ha pedido. Vayase en hora mala. "Ese es hombre que no tiene De caudal para una capa."	"Daughter, León has asked for your hand. Go away this fateful hour. This is a man without any means to clothe himself."
"Padre casame con el Y aunque nunca me deis nada." "Ke los bienes deste mundo Dios los daba y los quitaba."	"Father let me marry him and I will never ask anything more." "God gives you all the good things in this world and he takes them away."
Ahi concio Don Pedro Ke de amores se trataba Alquiló quatro valientes, Los mayores de la playa	But Don Pedro knew how to deal with the lovers. He hired four strong men, the best on the coast,
Ke ande encontrén a León Ke le sacaran el alma. A la subida de un monte con los quatro se encontrara.	to go and find León and frighten him away. They would find him on the top of a mountain.
León que se vio sin armas A la mar se tira y nada. Unos dicen que murió Diós le perdone su alma.	León they saw unarmed and he threw himself into the sea. Some thought he died but God saved his soul.
Otros dicen que le vieron A la otra parte del agua. No son tres dias pasados León en la playa estaba.	Others said that they saw him on another side of the water. Hardly three days had gone by; León was on the beach.
Por donde fuera a pasar? Por la calle de su dama, mi dama que no responde parece que esta trocada	Where had he been? Along the street where his lady lived, my lady who doesn't answer. It seems she has changed her mind.
"No estoy trocada León. Que aun estoy en mi palavra." Abajo las escaleras Como una leona brava. Y otro dia en la mañana Las ricas bodas se armaran	"I haven't changed my mind, Leon. I still stand by my word." She flew down the stairs like a brave lioness. The next day in the morning they were united at a lavish wedding.

3. Your teacher will assign each of you a verse number.

On a blank sheet of paper write one sentence in large letters summarizing that verse. (You may simplify it)

4. Select a member of the class to play each of the following:

   A. Diego León
   B. The young lady, Dona Juana
   C. The father, Don Pedro
   D-G. The four strong men

   These 7 actors should then go to the front of the class.

5. Fourteen of the remaining students should be chosen to represent each of the 14 numbered verses. Taking along their papers, they should then line up in order (from 1 to 14) down the side of the classroom.

   The actors should now be standing in front of the class.
   The students representing each verse should be lined up along of the side.

   PLAY THE SONG AGAIN .

   The person with the sentence for that particular verse should hold it up high so the actors can read it.
   The actors should mime the action they see on the sheets of paper.
   Continue through all 14 verses as you hear them in the song.

   NOTE: After each student has held a paper up high, he or she should turn it towards the class.

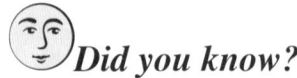*Did you know?*

There is a crater on the moon named after Alfonso X. It is called Alfonsus.

Lesson 5

A Horrible Time

Jews had lived in Spain since the time of the Romans, and perhaps even earlier when they may have come there with the Phoenician traders. They had helped to develop its culture and economy. They had enjoyed glorious years during the time when the Muslims ruled most of Spain. But as the Christians re-conquered the Iberian peninsula, more and more of the local people wanted the area to become an all-Christian land. In earlier years they were prized for their ability to deal with the Muslims and for their merchant skills. Now they were no longer needed. So, in 1492, after a great victory over the Muslims at Granada, King Ferdinand and Queen Isabella, decided to expel the Jews.

WHAT COULD THEY DO?

As the year **1492** approaches we consider what it must have felt like to be in Spain.

The Christians are finally gaining control of the Muslim part of Spain. There is a rising tide of anti-Jewish feeling not only in Spain but the whole of Europe. In the last 100 years alone there have been horrific incidents in Spain:

The Jews have been falsely accused of outrageous acts. For example:

1. Poisoning wells.
2. Mocking Christianity by stamping on the Cross.
3. Killing Christian babies and using their blood to make matzot.

converso is the name used for Jews who were forced to convert. We will see the word again and again in our series. Some people also call them **marranos.**

As a result of persecutions, many Jews convert. They are called *converso*s.

Some of the Old Christians are still uneasy. They say that since the *converso*s do not have "pure Christian blood" they should not hold the really important jobs. Moreover, now that the Christians have re-conquered all of the Muslim territories in Spain, they are ready to think about getting rid of the Jews altogether.

Finally, King Ferdinand and Queen Isabella decide to pass the Edict of Expulsion. They **sign** it in the Alhambra Palace on March 31, 1492.

You can still visit the room in the Alhambra Palace where the edict was signed

"All Jews must convert or leave within four months!"

TASK 1.

Use the newspaper articles on the next page as if they were the scripts of a TV news broadcast like CNN. Appoint two news anchors to sit at a table facing the class. Two other members of the class become the reporters in the field: one in Segovia and the other in Cordoba. They sit at the sides of the room.

The anchors read the news reports except for the on-site reports from Segovia and Cordoba. These are read out loud by the reporters.

NOW TURN TO *The Spanish Times...*

The Spanish Times

Alhambra, 1492

Jews Who Refuse To Convert Prepare For Expulsion

Time is running short and a lot has happened. The Edict of expulsion signed by Fernando and Isabella in March explicitly stated that "All Jews and Jewesses of whatever age who reside in our domains and territories... must leave with their sons and daughters, their servants and their relatives by the end of July and that they dare not return to our lands. Any Jew who does not comply or returns to our kingdom will incur punishment by death."

Abraham Seneor Converts

Abraham Seneor, the Chief Tax Collector and leader of the Jews, converted yesterday and was baptized at the high altar. Friends say Queen Isabella swore to destroy all Spanish Jews if he refused.

Pirates seen off Africa

Jews making for the port of Cadiz to board boats to North Africa are warned pirates are poised off shore to rob them.

We prefer to convert!

Dozens of Jews are converting to protect their jobs and their wives and children rather than risk losing everything.

Teresa de León's Agony
By Our Reporter in Segovia

I watched helplessly as Teresa de León, a Jew in this town noted for her skills as a dressmaker, placed her elderly father on the back of a hay cart filled with clothing and food. Her sick father begged her to leave him there to die, but she insisted saying, "all of us go, or we do not go at all." Then she slowly walked up to her front door and took the mezuzah from the doorpost. She reached into her pocket, pulled out a large iron key and locked the door securely. She walked back to the wagon and gave the key to her son-in-law.

"Jacob," she said, "this has been the key to our house for as long as I can remember. We have many beautiful memories of the time we spent here, especially when my husband, Jaimito, of blessed memory, was still alive. I want you to have this key. I want you to keep it and treasure it and save it for your children and your children's children. Let it be a reminder to all the generations that come after us of what we once had in Spain."

Jews Struggle Towards Ports and the Portugal Frontier

With the boiling hot sun beating down on them, processions of Jews with all their belongings trudge wearily, mile after mile, along the roads to the ports and frontiers. They sleep in fields. Some collapse on the way. Old men die and babies are born under the open skies. Urged on by the rabbis, women and girls sing and play tambourines to keep their spirits up.

Jews' Houses and Vineyards Sold for Price of a Donkey
By Our Reporter in Cordoba

A little boy called Julio from Cordoba was discovered burying his chess pieces and silver star of David in the hope he would come back to Spain. Tearfully, he told how his father had sold his vineyard and said that the money they got for it was only enough to buy a donkey. The Catholics, he explained, had raised their prices when they saw how badly the Jews needed the donkeys.

Many Converted Jews who continue Old Habits

Even though Isaac Bravel, a shoemaker from Granada, became a Catholic a month ago, he was still seen closing his stall on Saturdays as if he were still a Jew. "This behavior will not be tolerated," said the King. "Those who are still found to be saying Jewish prayers or observing Jewish rituals will be burnt at the stake in the great plazas of our beloved cities."

TASK 2: The class divides into two groups. One group represents Jews who are leaving. The other represents Jews who decide to convert and stay. There are two sets of questions: *leaving* or *staying.* Using the information in the newspaper, answer the questions that apply to your group in the space below. Then discuss as a class.

LEAVING	STAYING
Why have you decided to leave?	Why are you converting and staying?
What items will you take with you?	Will you still be a Jew in secret? How?
What dangers do you face?	What punishment could you face if you are caught behaving like a Jew?
Write down two words to describe how you feel	Write down two words to describe how you feel